A JUST BOX?

By Goldie Taub Chernoff

Pictures by Margaret Hartelius

D1377311

SCHOLASTIC BOOK SERVICES
NEW YORK · TORONTO · LONDON · AUCKLAND · SYDNEY · TOKYO

a box can be a BASKET

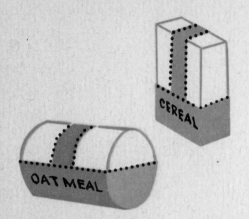

CEREAL

OAT MEAL

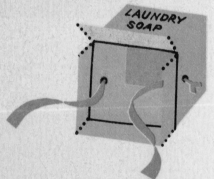

LAUNDRY SOAP

- Cut slits in each corner.
- Fold out for brim.
- Punch holes on each side. Push ribbon through holes and knot as shown.
- Decorate.

a HAT

SUGAR

Decorate.

SALT

Decorate.

a DICKEY BIRD

a ZOO

CAGE

Make bars from yarn or strips of paper. Glue or tape over opening as shown.

LION

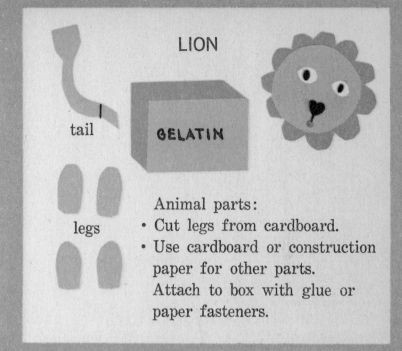

Animal parts:
- Cut legs from cardboard.
- Use cardboard or construction paper for other parts. Attach to box with glue or paper fasteners.

ALLIGATOR

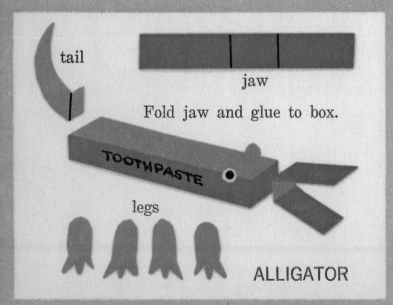

Fold jaw and glue to box.

ELEPHANT

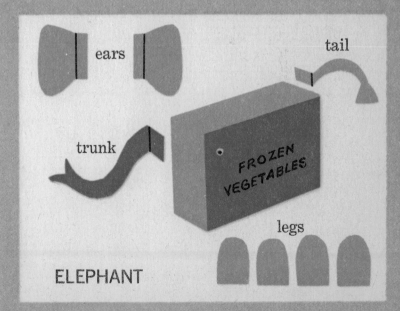

a CANOE

TEPEES

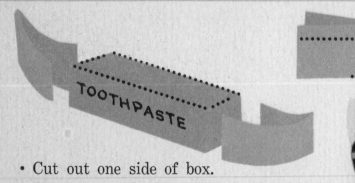

- Cut out one side of box.
- Cut canoe ends from folded paper.
  Glue in place.
- Cut Indian from paper.
  Fold and glue to bottom of canoe.

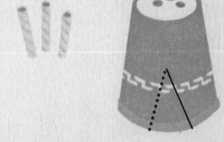

- Punch 3 holes in cup.
- Cut drinking straw in 3 pieces.
  Insert in holes.
- Cut flap, fold back.

a TOTEM POLE

a MASK

SMALL CEREAL

COOKIES

CRACKERS

FIG NEWTONS

OAT MEAL

Decorate boxes.
Glue together.

Cut on dotted line..........
Fold on solid line_____

- Cut away back and one end of box.
- Punch holes on each side. Push ribbon or cord through holes and knot.
- Cut out holes for eyes.
- Make nose flap by cutting on 3 sides as shown.
- Decorate.

BACK

CEREAL

FRONT

a box can be a HORSE

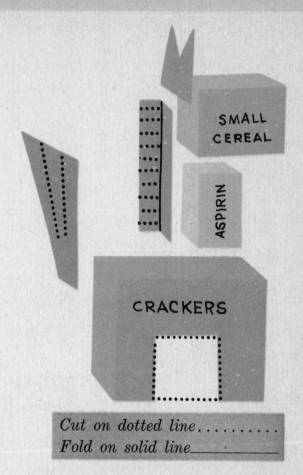

SMALL CEREAL

ASPIRIN

CRACKERS

Cut on dotted line..........
Fold on solid line_____

- Body and legs: Cut opening in box as shown.
  Repeat on opposite side.
- Neck: Glue aspirin box to cracker box. Let dry.
- Head: Glue small cereal box to neck.
- Cut mane, tail, and ears out of construction paper. Glue in place.

PUPPETS

HAND PUPPET

Cut box on 3 sides.
Fold on fourth side as shown.
Decorate.

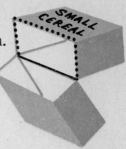

Move fingers and thumb to make puppet "talk."

STICK PUPPET

- Punch hole in box.
- Insert stick or pencil in hole.
- Decorate.

a STAGE

CARTON

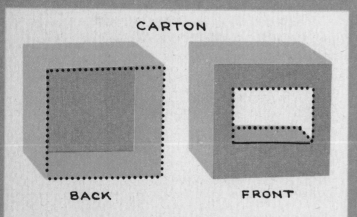

BACK

FRONT

Remove back of carton.
Cut opening on 3 sides.
Fold flap back for stage.

CARTON

Cut on dotted line . . . .
Fold on solid line _____

an EASEL

a
box
can
be

a STORE

a CASTLE

Roof: Cut semicircle from paper.
Overlap ends to form cone. Glue.

Tower: Oatmeal box.
Glue on paper windows.

Middle section:
Large laundry soap
or cereal box.

- Glue on paper windows.
- Cut out door. Fold back.

Bottom section: Large carton.
- Cut out drawbridge. Fold down.
- Draw lines on box for parapet.

a VILLAGE

Use construction paper for
roofs, doors, windows,
and chimneys.
Glue in place.

MILK CARTON

SMALL CEREAL

COOKIE BOX

Cut out store window
on 3 sides.
Fold to form awning.

a DOLL HOUSE

CARTON

Roof: Use construction paper or cardboard folded in half. Fold ends to form flaps. Cut 2 slits in roof. Insert match-box lid or other box in slits to form chimney. Glue roof to house.

- Leave flaps on carton.
- Cut out door as shown.
- Cut openings for windows or make paper windows and glue them on.

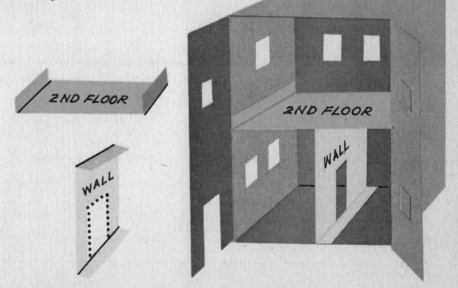

2ND FLOOR

WALL

2ND FLOOR

WALL

2nd floor and wall: Use piece of cardboard slightly larger than box. Fold ends up. Cut out door in wall as shown. Glue in place.

BUNK BED

TIES

- Cut the box and cover in half. Use cover halves for head and foot boards. Use box halves for upper and lower bunks.
- Glue bunks in place as shown.

DOLLS' BEDS

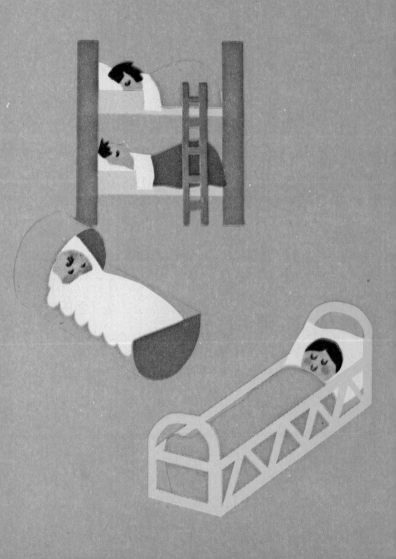

CRADLE

OAT MEAL

Cut on dotted line.........

TOMATO CARTON

TABLES

TABLE

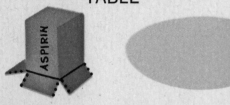

- Remove bottom flaps from aspirin box.
- Cut slits in corners and fold out flaps as shown.
- Glue cardboard table top in place.

SNACK BAR

Cut away top and one side of box.

STOOLS

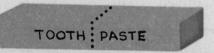

and CHAIRS

boxes can be TRAINS

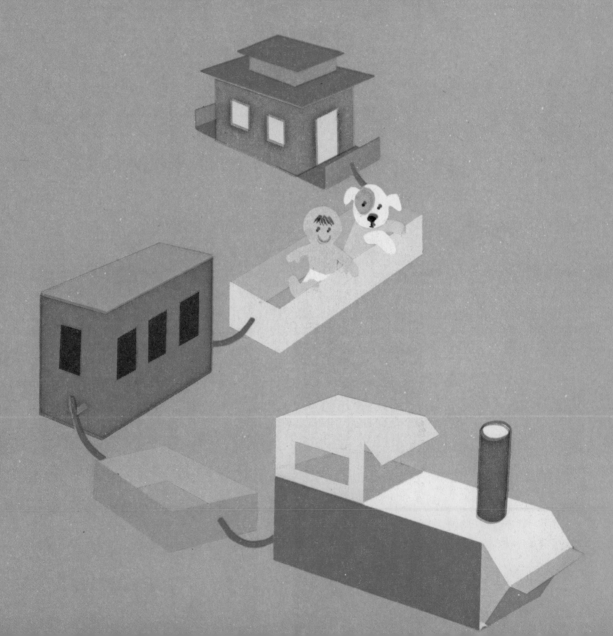

CABOOSE

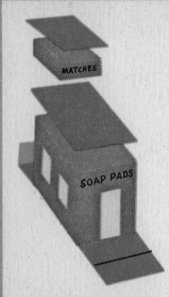

- Cut out or glue on doors and windows.
- Make flat roofs from construction paper and glue to boxes.
- Glue boxes together.
- Cut long cardboard strip for platform. Fold ends up. Glue to bottom of caboose.

Cut on dotted line. . . . .
Fold on solid line_____

FLAT CAR
- Punch holes at ends of each car.
- Link all cars together with knotted cord as shown.

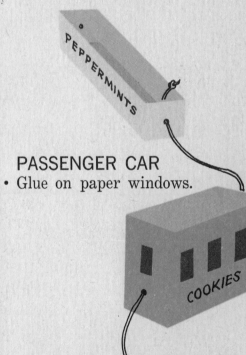

PASSENGER CAR
- Glue on paper windows.

ENGINE

- Cut out windows on each side of small cereal box.
- Cut front on 3 sides. Fold flap up. Glue to carton.
- Glue bouillon box to milk carton.

COAL CAR

BOATS

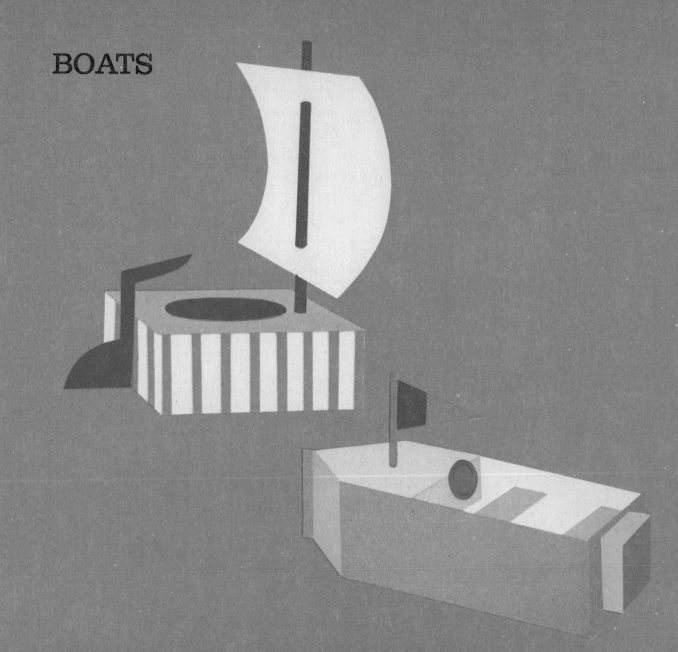

SAILBOAT

- Insert drinking straw through paper for mast and sail.
- Make hole in box and insert straw.

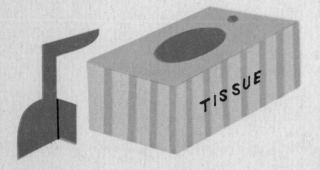

- Cut rudder out of cardboard.
- Glue flap of rudder to box.

MOTORBOAT

- Cut out side of carton as shown.
- Fold down flap for dashboard.
- Steering wheel: Glue button to dashboard.

- Seats: Fold ends on strip of cardboard. Glue in place as shown.
- Motor: Glue small match box to milk carton.
- Flag: Insert toothpick through decorated paper.

PLANES

HELICOPTER

Propellers: Cut cardboard strips
for blades. (Cover with foil if
desired.) Fold drinking straw
at one end. Insert straight pin
through centers of blades and
bent end of straw.
Insert in holes.
Glue on paper windows and doors.

JET

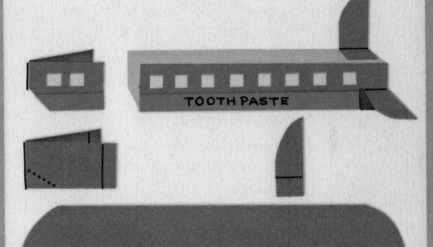

- Glue paper windows in place on sides
  of long box.
- Nose: Fold a strip of construction
  paper in half. Fold ends back to
  form flaps. Glue to box as shown.
- Tail: Cut 3 identical pieces out of
  construction paper as shown. Fold
  flaps and glue to box as shown.
- Wings: Cut a long strip of construction paper, curving the front as
  shown. Glue to underbody.

WANT SOME MORE IDEAS? TRY THESE.

BOOK ENDS— Fill two sturdy boxes with stones, bricks, or sand. Seal and decorate.

COSTUME— Cut an opening at the end of a large carton for a head to go through. Decorate.

MOBILE— Suspend a variety of small boxes and shapes from a rod at different levels.

PHOTO CUBE— Glue family photos around five sides of a square box.

PIÑATA— On birthdays or holidays, fill a large, lightweight decorated box with little toys and gifts. Seal and use in piñata game.

STRING DESIGNS— Notch the edges of a box. Secure the end of a long piece of string in one of the notches. Then stretch the string up, down, and across catching the string in the notches.

You can decorate the things you make with crayons, felt tip markers, poster paint, spray paint, decorative tape, yarn, scraps of colored paper, tin foil, cloth, wallpaper, magazine ads, buttons and beads — or anything else that strikes your imagination.

Here's a suggestion: If you want to paint a waxy or glassy surface, first rub the area with a soapy cloth.